MAY 1 7 2017

SPOTLIGHT ON ECOLOGY AND LIFE SCIENCE

INTERDEPENDENCE OF SPECIES

ELLIOT MONROE

PowerKiDS press™

NEW YORK

Published in 2017 by The Rosen Publishing Group, Inc.
29 East 21st Street, New York, NY 10010

Editor: Melissa Raé Shofner
Book Design: Michael Flynn
Interior Layout: Reann Nye

Photo Credits: Cover eli_asenova/E+/Getty Images; p. 5 Frans Lanting/Mint Images/Getty Images; p. 7 Buyenlarge/ Archive Photos/Getty Images; p. 9 (rabbit) Tom Middleton/Shutterstock.com; p. 9 (mouse) Rudmer Zwerver/ Shutterstock; p. 9 (deer) Tony Campbell/Shutterstock.com; p. 9 (owl) Don Mammoser/Shutterstock.com; p. 9 (coyote) Josef Pittner/Shutterstock.com; p. 9 (grass) biletskiy/Shutterstock.com; p. 10 Bruno Roza/ Shutterstock.com; p. 11 Smith Collection/Gado/Archive Photos/Getty Images; p. 13 Ondrej Prosicky/ Shutterstock.com; p. 14 Print Collector/Hulton Archive/Getty Images; p. 15 dilynn/Shutterstock.com; p. 17 Villiers Steyn/Shutterstock.com; p. 18 jeep2499/Shutterstock.com; p. 19 Barcroft/Barcroft Media/ Getty Images; p. 21 DOMINIQUE FAGET/AFP/Getty Images; p. 22 Lucian Coman/Shutterstock.com.

Cataloging-in-Publication Data

Names: Monroe, Elliot.
Title: Interdependence of species / Elliot Monroe.
Description: New York : PowerKids Press, 2017. | Series: Spotlight on ecology and life science | Includes index.
Identifiers: ISBN 9781499425956 (pbk.) | ISBN 9781499425987 (library bound) | ISBN 9781499425963 (6 pack)
Subjects: LCSH: Ecology--Juvenile literature. | Biotic communities--Juvenile literature. | Food chains (Ecology)-- Juvenile literature.
Classification: LCC QH541.14 M66 2017 | DDC 577--dc23

Manufactured in China

CPSIA Compliance Information: Batch #BW17PK For further information contact Rosen Publishing, New York, New York at 1-800-237-9932.

CONTENTS

FRIEND OR FOE? 4

NATURE'S NEIGHBORHOODS 6

MAKING CONNECTIONS 8

SPECIES SYMBIOSIS 10

PARTNERS AND PALS 12

ROOMMATES 14

VAMPIRES AND CUCKOOS 16

COMFORTABLE COMPANIONS 18

PEOPLE'S PART TO PLAY 20

HELPING HANDS 22

GLOSSARY 23

INDEX 24

PRIMARY SOURCE LIST 24

WEBSITES 24

CHAPTER ONE

FRIEND OR FOE?

Scientists believe there are about 8.7 million **species** on Earth. About 1.2 million species have been discovered so far, and new species continue to be named. Each species has special qualities that make it unlike any other. How do these neighbors on planet Earth deal with each other? Do they fight or work together? Do they share the relationship of partners or of predators and **prey**?

The varied interactions of Earth's species are all part of the balance of the natural world. Through the simple act of survival, from birth to death, each **organism** affects the lives of many other organisms.

Interdependence describes the way that plant and animal species rely, or depend, on one another to survive. Different species depend on each other for food and shelter. Some even work together to avoid predators. By exploring the special relationships of these species, we can begin to understand the connections between all of Earth's creatures.

Each species is important and has something special to offer.

CHAPTER TWO

NATURE'S NEIGHBORHOODS

Each species is part of an ecosystem. An ecosystem is the community of living creatures and nonliving things in an **environment**. Living creatures could be plants such as grass or trees or animals such as insects, birds, or deer. Nonliving elements of an ecosystem include water, soil, temperature, and sunlight. Both living and nonliving things are needed for an ecosystem to function.

Ecosystems vary depending on their location. An Arctic ecosystem usually supports few species of plants and animals, while a rain forest is home to many. The healthiest ecosystems are those where many different species live. Biodiversity refers to the amount of different species in an ecosystem. Since different plants and animals have different parts to play, biodiversity helps ecosystems maintain balance. The greater the amount of species, the more interactions there are between them.

German biologist Ernst Haeckel studied hundreds of species of organisms. His illustrations of plant and animal species were published in a book of prints called *Kunstformen der Natur (Art Forms in Nature)*.

CHAPTER THREE

MAKING CONNECTIONS

All species in an ecosystem are connected by the transfer, or movement, of energy through a food chain. A food chain shows how species are connected based on what they eat. The three basic levels of a food chain are producer, consumer, and decomposer.

Plants are producers because they use nonliving elements of the ecosystem, such as sunlight, to get the energy they need to grow and live. A consumer is an animal that eats other organisms to survive. There are different levels of consumers. Some eat only plants, while some eat other consumers. A decomposer is an organism that breaks down the bodies of dead producers and consumers. This recycles **nutrients** back into the ecosystem.

The entire ecosystem is based on these relationships. If the population of one species is at risk, it puts all the other species in the food chain at risk, too.

GRASSES

WHITE-TAILED DEER

FIELD MOUSE

RABBIT

BARRED OWL

COYOTE

An ecosystem doesn't have just one food chain but several that operate at the same time. A food web shows how species are connected by the different paths of energy in each chain.

CHAPTER FOUR

SPECIES SYMBIOSIS

No matter their place in the food chain, each species in an ecosystem affects the others. Species compete for food or shelter and rely on each other for **resources**. You've probably seen a bird nesting in a tree, a bee visiting a flower, or a flea sticking on a dog. These are examples of symbiosis. Symbiosis is a close relationship between two different species.

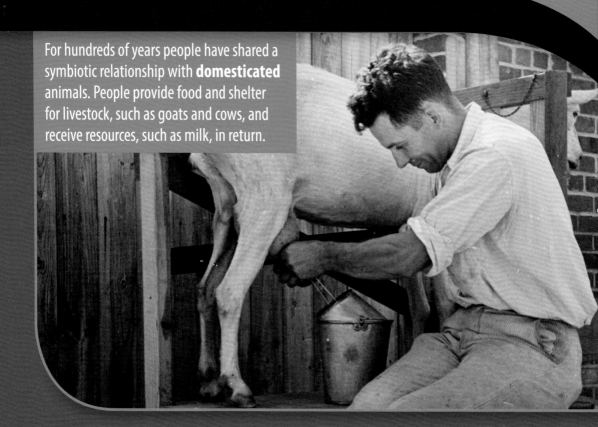

For hundreds of years people have shared a symbiotic relationship with **domesticated** animals. People provide food and shelter for livestock, such as goats and cows, and receive resources, such as milk, in return.

Symbiotic relationships are usually thought of as being beneficial to both species involved. However, not all of them are. Different types of symbiosis include mutualism, commensalism, and parasitism. When both species benefit from their symbiotic relationship it's called mutualism. Commensalism occurs when one species benefits from the interaction and the other isn't affected. When one species benefits but the other suffers, it's known as parasitism. These symbiotic behaviors give us a glimpse of how species depend on one another for survival.

CHAPTER FIVE

PARTNERS AND PALS

Can plants and animals be pals? Maybe they're not friends, but species that practice mutualism do work together as partners!

Flowering plants need help spreading their pollen to produce new plants. Flowers **attract** bees with nectar, which is a sugary, sweet juice that bees collect and use to make honey. Bees are called pollinators because they spread pollen as they fly from flower to flower. Without the help of pollinators, flowering plants wouldn't be able to create offspring. Without the nectar provided by flowers, bees wouldn't be able to create honey. Bees and plants cooperate, or work together, which is necessary for the survival of both species.

Acacia trees share a similarly beneficial relationship with ants. Ants are drawn to acacia trees by the sweet nectar they produce. In return for nectar, ants protect acacia trees from **herbivores** and other plants.

Hummingbirds, butterflies, and moths are also helpful pollinators for flowering plants.

CHAPTER SIX

ROOMMATES

A sea anemone is a soft-bodied ocean animal that looks like a flower. Clown fish like to live in and around anemones. Anemones have stinging **tentacles**, which protect clown fish from predators. In return for shelter and protection, clown fish clean parasites from an anemone's body. They also protect anemones from predators that try to eat their tentacles.

SEA ANEMONES

The Gila woodpecker nests in the holes of a saguaro cactus. Their relationship is mutualistic. The cactus's spines protect the woodpecker from predators. The woodpecker eats harmful insects that prey on the cactus.

Pistol shrimp are master diggers. They make tunnels in the sand where they can hide from predators. Unfortunately, pistol shrimp have very poor eyesight. Luckily, they can rely on gobies to let them know when danger is coming. Gobies are small fish that live on the ocean floor. They see better than pistol shrimp but aren't as skilled at digging burrows. The two creatures partner up to use each other's strengths to their mutual advantage. They share a burrow, communicating with their antennae and tail.

CHAPTER SEVEN

VAMPIRES AND CUCKOOS

Nobody wants to cross paths with a parasite. These creatures are harmful to their hosts, taking what they need without giving any benefits back.

The cuckoo bird is considered a parasite. Instead of caring for its own young, it lays its eggs in the nests of other birds. The cuckoo will remove eggs that belong in the nest, hoping that its own eggs will go unnoticed by the parents who raise the chicks as their own. Since cuckoo young are sometimes larger than their nest neighbors, they can push smaller birds out after they've hatched.

Freshwater leeches are nature's vampires. They hook their sharp teeth into their victims and suck their blood! Leeches can drink up to five times their weight in blood in a single feeding. Luckily, they don't need to eat very often. They can wait up to a year between feedings.

Oxpeckers ride on the back of large animals, such as impalas, eating the ticks and flies on their hides. Unfortunately, they also suck the blood of their hosts. Their relationship is a blend of mutualism and parasitism.

CHAPTER EIGHT

COMFORTABLE COMPANIONS

A barnacle is an ocean animal related to lobsters and crabs. These strange little creatures stand on their heads and eat with their feet, but they can't move on their own. Barnacles rely on other animals to provide a place for them to live.

When they're young, barnacles float until they find a good surface to attach themselves to. Once latched on to a surface, barnacles form a hard outer shell that glues them

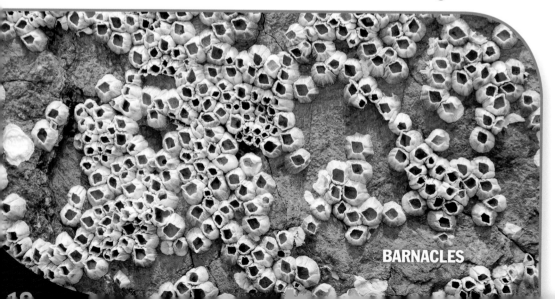

BARNACLES

Barnacles share a relationship of commensalism with whales, benefiting from the interaction and leaving the whale unaffected.

securely in place. Thin, leglike tentacles stretch out from the shell to catch food from the surrounding water.

Barnacles may fix themselves to crabs, the shells of sea turtles, and the bodies of whales. Most barnacles are harmless. The creatures they live on may not even know they're there! Humpback and gray whales are the most popular hosts and have been known to carry hundreds of pounds of barnacles.

CHAPTER NINE

PEOPLE'S PART TO PLAY

Consider the ways humans depend on other species to survive. We rely on plants to provide us with food and the resources needed to build shelters and tools. We depend on animals as sources of meat, milk, eggs, and other foods. We also use them to help us work and keep them as pets.

Humans are at the very top of the food chain. Although we depend heavily on the resources that plants and animals provide, we haven't done our best to contribute to the ecosystem in return.

People put the balance of biodiversity in danger by building over ecosystems, overhunting animals, polluting the environment, and using too many resources. The human population has grown so much that space for wildlife has become limited. When a plant or animal species becomes **endangered** because of human activities, the other species that depend on it are also at risk.

Greenpeace is a global group of people working together to protect the environment from pollution and **destruction**. Members take part in peaceful protests to raise awareness about environmental issues.

CHAPTER TEN

HELPING HANDS

By changing how we think about the natural world, humans can create a healthier relationship with other species. Instead of overusing resources and destroying ecosystems, we should value plants and animals. How can we give back to the species we depend on?

Planting a garden helps all the species in your ecosystem, from the bees that drink nectar to the people and animals that breathe oxygen released by plants. By caring for your plants by watering them and removing weeds, you can share mutualistic relationships with other species.

Most importantly, we can **conserve** resources in the environment. Reuse and recycle products such as paper, plastic, and glass, and reduce the amount of water you use. People are just one species in a world of millions, and we all depend on one another to survive.

GLOSSARY

attract (uh-TRAKT) To draw toward.

conserve (kun-SERV) To keep something from harm and not waste it.

destruction (dih-STRUK-shun) Great damage or ruin.

domesticated (duh-MES-tih-kay-tuhd) Bred and raised for use by people.

endangered (in-DAYN-juhrd) In danger of dying out.

environment (en-VY-run-muhnt) The conditions that surround a living thing and affect the way it lives.

herbivore (ER-buh-vor) An animal that eats plants.

nutrient (NOO-tree-uhnt) Something taken in by a plant or animal that helps it grow and stay healthy.

organism (OR-guh-nih-zuhm) An individual living thing.

prey (PRAY) An animal hunted by other animals for food.

resource (REE-sors) Something that can be used.

species (SPEE-sheez) A group of plants or animals that are all the same kind.

tentacle (TEN-tuh-kul) A long, thin body part that sticks out from an animal's head or mouth.

INDEX

A
anemone, sea, 14
ants, 12

B
barnacle, 18, 19
bees, 10, 12
biodiversity, 6, 20
butterfly, 13

C
cactus, saguaro, 15
clown fish, 14
commensalism, 11, 19
consumer, 8
coyote, 9
cuckoo, 16

D
decomposer, 8
deer, white-tailed, 9

E
ecosystem, 6, 8, 9, 10, 20, 22

F
flowers, 10, 12
food chain, 8, 9, 10, 20
food web, 9

G
goby, 15
grass, 6, 9
Greenpeace, 21

H
Haeckel, Ernst, 7
hummingbird, 13

I
impala, 17

L
leeches, freshwater, 16

M
moth, 13
mouse, field, 9
mutualism, 11, 12, 15, 17, 22

O
owl, barred, 9
oxpecker, 17

P
parasitism, 11, 14, 16, 17
pollinator, 12, 13
producer, 8

R
rabbit, 8, 9

S
shrimp, pistol, 15
symbiosis, 10, 11

T
trees, 6, 10, 12

W
whale, 19
woodpecker, Gila, 15

PRIMARY SOURCE LIST

Page 7
Plate 99, Trochilidae. Lithographic print. Created by Ernst Haeckel. From *Kunstformen der Natur*. 1904.

Page 14
Sea anemones. Print. Created by A. Fullerton & Co. Held by Getty Images, Hulton Archive Collection. ca. 19th century.

Page 21
Greenpeace activists at a protest at the United Nations climate change conference. Photograph. By Dominique Faget/AFP/Getty Images. Taken in Le Bourget, France. December 9, 2015.

WEBSITES

Due to the changing nature of Internet links, PowerKids Press has developed an online list of websites related to the subject of this book. This site is updated regularly. Please use this link to access the list: www.powerkidslinks.com/sels/inter